THE 747:
A TUMULTUOUS BEGINNING

Flying Through Turbulence

RONALD MARASCO

All income from sales will be donated
to the Pan Am Historical Foundation
to promote and preserve the legacy of
the commercial jet age technical
accomplishments and the unique historical
experiences of maintenance, engineering
and flight operations.

ISBN: 1502782456
ISBN 13: 9781502782458

DEDICATION

To the people on the front line of the airline's operation during the 747's tumultuous beginning. Notably, the maintenance supervisors, mechanics, pilots, flight engineers and flight attendants and the support and ground staff who faced the passengers every day. And most especially Captain Jim Waugh, senior vice president of operations for Pan Am, a close friend and 747 pioneer aviator, who so greatly respected all of the aforementioned people.

Acknowledgement

Pete Runnette, Peter Leslie, Doug Miller and the Pan Am Historical Foundation for their support, Robert Gandt, Foundation Board member and noted author for his invaluable advice and editing, and Niels Anderson for salvaging the John Borger files.

CONTENTS

INTRODUCTION

Much has been written about the creation and development of the 747, and as the years roll on and anniversaries accumulate, there will be more stories about this storied airplane. It is true that Boeing and the engine manufacturer, Pratt & Whitney, overcame significant problems during the development of the aircraft. It is also true, but never mentioned, that the airlines also confronted *incredible* challenges throughout the 747's early operation.

The primary motivation for writing this narrative is to recount how thousands of airline people struggled mightily to ensure the 747's reliability and safety during the early years of the operation. Throughout the review I refer to the early years of the operation, because for many reasons it's hard to cite a specific number of years. Suffice it to say, the early years encompass a *long* period of time.

The 747 was plagued with serious in-flight incidents, overwhelmingly poor engine reliability, and numerous mechanical aircraft system problems from the beginning. Yet the written record of the aircraft's early operational history is non-existent. By law, flight safety and extraordinary ground maintenance problems must be reported and recorded, therefore the FAA, Boeing, and Pratt & Whitney should have this history somewhere in their archives. Absent those records, there are many eye-witness accounts which detail the aircraft's poor reliability. There are also extensive documents from the personal files of John Borger, Pan Am's Chief Engineer, with data and revealing correspondence which corroborate the 747's many reliability problems during this historical period.

One other objective for documenting this early history is to refresh the memories of those who were there at the beginning, and to introduce others to what a monumental event the 747 was in the context of history at that time. Unquestionably, the 747's technology was unprecedented and daunting. Indeed, from a business perspective it might have been one of the biggest private enterprise gambles of the twentieth century.

The ranks of those who actively participated in the introduction of the 747 are rapidly dwindling. Since I was fortunate to have a maintenance and operational vantage point that spanned the 747 operation from a few years before its start-up, until many years thereafter, it seemed appropriate to compile a collection of notes, observations and input from colleagues into a brief book. With the exception of a summary on the last few pages, it is in essence, a factual description of a never to be duplicated event in commercial aviation history.

THE UNTOLD STORY

The Boeing B747 was clearly years ahead of its time, and history has shown that it literally changed the world of commercial aviation overnight. Ironically, the many airline personnel involved in the early years of the operation probably never realized they were making history. While Pan American World Airways was by far the largest 747 operator in the world, TWA, British Airways, Lufthansa, and Japan Airlines also had formidable fleets. This provided a rare opportunity for airline people throughout the world to participate in the historic beginning of this magnificent aircraft.

Today the 747 is the majestic and reliable "Queen of the Sky," and the Boeing Company rightly deserves great credit for its masterpiece. But that company certainly does not deserve it all, because the airlines played a major role in navigating the 747 through a tumultuous beginning. The facts will show that after delivery to the airlines, the 747 did not simply live happily ever after.

The Boeing website for the early 747-100 classic airplane has considerable technical information and a description of the manufacturing challenges. Unfortunately, for whatever reason, there is no mention of the aircraft's service introduction history. The popular *Wikipedia* site has a complete narrative on the first 747s, but the W*ikipedia* description of the aircraft's service introduction alleges that "Although technical problems occurred, they were relatively minor and quickly solved." It's difficult to imagine where they got their information from, but nothing could be further from the truth.

The 747 did not simply have teething problems during its introduction. For well over two years, it had very serious in-flight incidents and maintenance problems that were persistent, caused disruptive passenger delays, and were extraordinarily costly. The purpose of this narrative is to tell the untold story of how the airlines overcame the enormous maintenance, flight operations, and reliability challenges during the early years of the operation. Further, it will chronicle their significant contributions toward the ultimate success of the 747. Riveting testimony and eyewitness accounts from people who had an array of engineering, technical, and flight operations responsibilities at the time will clearly demonstrate the crucial role of the airlines in propelling the Boeing 747 into the aviation icon it is today.

Included for additional reference are notes from the Pan Am Historical Foundation and documents from John Borger, Pan Am's chief engineer, who spearheaded the 747's development. Borger had an extensive collection of illuminating and insightful personal files, covering the 747's early years. Copies of documents that support the narrative in The Borger Files section are listed in the Appendix.

Since Pan Am was going to be awash with 747's the first year of operation, Jim Weesner, vice president of maintenance and engineering strongly felt there should be a separate maintenance department that specialized in 747 maintenance. I was fortunate to be appointed General Manger of 747 Maintenance a few years before the delivery of the first aircraft. The position entailed all facets of preparing for the aircraft's arrival and ultimately managing the 747 production organization. Subsequently, for many years I held senior positions responsible for all aspects of 747 maintenance. However, this narrative is based on my experiences during the 747's early years, when I was close to the operational details of our world-wide daily operation.

In addition, there are numerous references and quotes from *747: Creating the World's First Jumbo Jet and Other Adventures from a Life in Aviation,* by Joe Sutter, Boeing's 747 chief design engineer. Sutter's book is a spellbinding account of unrevealed details from a Boeing insider who oversaw all aspects of the 747 design. In his tell-it-like-it-was style, he explains many aspects of the program that were of great concern to many of us. Sutter also extols Juan Trippe, chairman of Pan American, for his vision and for Pan Am's major contribution in launching the 747 program. Sutter was a pure technical genius who told his upper management things they were not happy to hear. I've quoted him extensively.

Joe Sutter, Chief 747 Design Engineer

How It All Began

Odd as it might seem, the 747 was not a Boeing Company initiative, although the Boeing website on the 747's history would not give you that impression. Boeing had no 747 marketing program, no aircraft proposal, and little interest in a jumbo commercial jet. At that time in the mid 1960's their primary focus was on the supersonic transport (SST) and the air force C5A cargo aircraft. Unlike any other program for a commercial aircraft before or since, the Boeing 747 program was the result of the vision and constant prodding by essentially one person: Juan Trippe, chairman of Pan American World Airways. Trippe was the legendary aviation pioneer of almost everything important in international aviation, including the beginning of the commercial aviation jet age in 1958 with the purchase of the Boeing 707.

When Pan Am made a commitment to purchase the 707, Boeing had a prototype aircraft they could demonstrate and market. The 707 was a derivative of proven military technology, and the prototype shown below had actually been flying for some time.

By comparison, when Mr. Trippe began prodding Boeing to forge ahead with the development of a jumbo aircraft, that type of airplane was only a concept—simply a vision of a big transport airplane.

Mr. Trippe had decided that it was time to build a *really* big aircraft, one at least twice the size of anything flying at the time. Sutter wrote:

> *Juan Trippe's vision of a big airplane was enough of a challenge. To make matters worse, even more interesting, he wanted this big new airplane—now. His business instincts were telling him that Pan Am's intercontinental routes could use the added capacity of bigger airplanes as soon as we could get them. Starting with Pan Am's data points, I set my team to work doing preliminary parametric studies to generate airplane weight, size and performance figures. To build an airplane—two and a half times bigger than anything in existence. Pan Am was by far the most*

6

influential international airline back then. It had launched the 707 and would launch the 747 as our new airplane would be known when the program was started—that is if we could come up with something that Pan Am liked.

There are many stories about Trippe's discussions with Bill Allen, Boeing's chairman, of the need to build a jumbo aircraft. The oft quoted story is that Trippe said, "You build it—we'll buy it." John Borger, chief engineer for Pan Am, noted in his memo on "The Evolution of an Airplane" that "discussions continued during the fall, particularly between Messrs. Trippe of Pan Am and Allen of Boeing. This resulted in a letter of intent to buy 25 passenger airplanes, signed on December 22, 1965." At the signing there was no sleek model, nor even a sketch of what the aircraft would look like. The letter of intent to build and purchase the aircraft was barely more binding than two powerful aviation icons shaking hands.

Boeing was keenly aware that without Pan Am, the 747 program was going nowhere. Sutter wrote:

It was obvious to me that the Pan Am chairman wanted the new Boeing 747 to be an aerial ocean liner with tall sides punctuated by two parallel rows of windows like portholes. If he had his way, passengers viewing the 747 from the airport terminal would look out and see something suggestive of a ship. Thus my people began drawing up double decker fuselages.

These initial double-decker design discussions involved two complete floor levels extending the full length of the aircraft and should not be confused with what ultimately became the "upstairs" lounge. Sutter's team quickly determined that the double-decker fuselage would not work for two reasons: one, the difficulty of evacuating passengers from the upper deck, and two, the wing design complications for a short, fat fuselage. Boeing's top management was deeply concerned that Trippe would be so unhappy with a single-deck aircraft that he would scrap the program and seek other manufacturers like Lockheed or Douglas. Boeing subsequently sent Milt Heinemann, a highly regarded interior design engineer, to New York to sell Trippe and his staff on the single-deck concept.

To emphasize the fuselage width of a single-deck 747 cabin, Heinemann took a twenty-foot coil of clothesline from his briefcase and stretched it across the boardroom. This graphic demonstration allowed the audience to envision how such a wide cabin floor area could accommodate very creative interior configurations. After many discussions and reviews on passenger capacity and various seat configurations, Trippe and his chief engineer, John Borger, approved. Thus was the single-deck, wide-bodied, two-aisle cabin configuration was born. This was a significant event in the history of commercial aviation—a design concept that would ultimately come to dominate today's world of long-range, wide-bodied, two-aisle, twin-engine aircraft.

These discussions also prompted a review of how to best utilize the floor space just aft of the cockpit. In the proposed fuselage design, in order to accommodate a main-deck cargo configuration, the cockpit was raised and the classic, top-of-the-fuselage hump was created aft of the cockpit. This afforded an upper-deck space for—something. When Trippe was told it would be a great crew rest facility, he said, "Rest area? This is going to be reserved for passengers!" Thus was born the legendary upper-deck lounge and spiral staircase—an eye-popping attraction for passengers walking through the 747 for the first time. And over the years the upper-deck lounge and the top fuselage hump grew in size to accommodate a wide variety of creative seating configurations.

Original Wide-Bodied Economy Configuration

Spiral Staircase to Upper-Deck Lounge

Upper-Deck Lounge

Curiously, the Boeing historical web site's description of *How It All Began* is contrary to the facts as we know them and as stated in the Sutter book. Boeing gives the impression that they had thousands of employees assigned to the 747 project and that "the incentive for creating the giant 747 came from reductions in air fares, a surge in passenger traffic and increasingly crowded skies." Sadly, Boeing did not give any credit where credit was due. There is little doubt that Juan Trippe changed the course of commercial aviation by single-handedly driving the development of the 747. Without Trippe there would be no 747 as we know it today.

In Sutter's postscript to his book he indicated that he (Sutter) is not the "only father" of the 747. "The 747 has three fathers," he wrote, "the other two being Juan Trippe of Pan American World Airways and Boeing's Bill Allen." A powerful statement by someone who was vastly aware of the facts, yet willing to share credit with the pivotal people associated with the 747 launch.

Because of Pan Am's status as a leading international airline, no airline wanted to be left behind. Even airlines with route structures not requiring a 747 ordered these innovative new aircraft. Unquestionably, the Pan Am order was the major catalyst for the stampede of airline orders that made it financially possible for Boeing to launch the program.

Bill Allen, Chairman of Boeing and Juan Trippe

THE 747's INTIMIDATING PHYSICAL SIZE

While age has a way of dimming the details of important events in our lives, it's fair to say that none of us will ever forget the first time we saw the 747. Unless you have passed the age sixty milestone, it's tough to fathom just how unbelievable the 747's size was relative to any other commercial jet aircraft in 1970. It was a show stopper. During the first years of the operation, people throughout the world flocked to airports just to see the 747 taxiing, taking off, or landing. Pan Am conducted dozens of tours especially for schoolchildren when the 747 was undergoing service. For the kids it was like a trip to Disneyland.

The airplane was two and a half times the size of anything flying at the time. Seeing the 747 for the first time was like coming out to your car in the morning to find it had grown to two and one half times its size. The cockpit was three stories above the ground, and pilots felt like they were taxiing or landing an aircraft from the third floor of a building; the tail's vertical stabilizer was five stories high. There was no limit to the words used to describe the 747's size. Even experienced airline people questioned whether it would actually fly.

747 vs 707
Everett, WA

Because no airline or airport in the world had facilities or equipment that could either maintain an aircraft that size or service its passengers, the 747 spawned a planning and facility-building frenzy throughout the world that has not been seen before or since. It was remarkable that the aviation world would spend millions of dollars on facilities and tooling without ever (1) seeing a completed aircraft or (2) being assured the aircraft would fly and be successful. It was truly a leap of faith.

My initial introduction to the size of the aircraft was in early 1968 during a visit to Boeing's plant in Everett, Washington. Everett was forty miles north of Seattle and would become the assembly facility for the 747. Boeing constructed what was then advertised as the largest building in the world, which was duly noted in *The Guinness Book of Records*.

Boeing had built a full-size mock-up of the aircraft in a corner of the plant. As Bob Blake, Pan Am's Boeing representative, described it, "The building was empty except for one walled off corner. As you entered the building the lobby was lined with drawings and production charts. There was a small entry door to the assembly section of the building and when you stepped through the door there it was—this monstrous full size aluminum and wood mock-up of the 747!" At first sight of the mock-up, most everyone expressed their shock in an array of expletives. One of the more famous repeated ones was "Holy sh—!" Seeing the airplane for the first time was a wake-up call and gave real insight to what lay ahead. Up until then the 747 had just been a planning manual.

The aircraft's sheer size would obviously complicate maintenance. Mechanics had to climb something to get to something in order to service just about anything. Whereas one person could service items on the 707, the 747 took two or more people. The access stands, special tooling, and lift equipment for units like the engine were overwhelming and complex. And of course everything was *big*.

Unprecedented New Technology

Before the 747, advancements in aircraft and engine technology were usually modest, incremental improvements. But the 747, which Boeing called "the new technology airplane," was anything but a modest technical advancement. It was a quantum leap in technology. Even for technical people who were well schooled on the 707, the 747's technology within the context of its time was positively breathtaking.

For the first time in commercial aviation history, all of the aircraft's flight controls were operated hydraulically. Without hydraulic power the aircraft could not be flown, so there were four hydraulic systems, plus standby and auxiliary hydraulic systems. Heretofore, all airliners had two main landing gear and eight wheels and brakes. The 747 had four main landing gears and sixteen wheels and brakes. The aircraft incorporated a sprawling, sophisticated three-slot, trailing-edge flap system. Suffice it to say, the list of "new technology airplane" systems was long and complex.

After an exhaustive study, Boeing chose the JT9D turbofan engine manufactured by Pratt & Whitney. The engine utilized revolutionary high-bypass technology in which the core jet engine drove a massive turbofan like a large propeller. The JT9D produced almost two and a half times more thrust (power) than any engine flying at the time. The physical size of the engine was staggering, and the technology groundbreaking. As previously mentioned, the increased engine thrust required to power the 747 was not simply a modest, incremental advancement. It was truly monumental, as revealed in the following JT9D cutaway showing the inside of the engine and in the 707-versus-747 engine thrust graph. Clearly, in order to meet the required thrust levels, the JT9D was pushing the design temperatures of the metals in the high-stage turbine.

JT9D Engine Cutaway

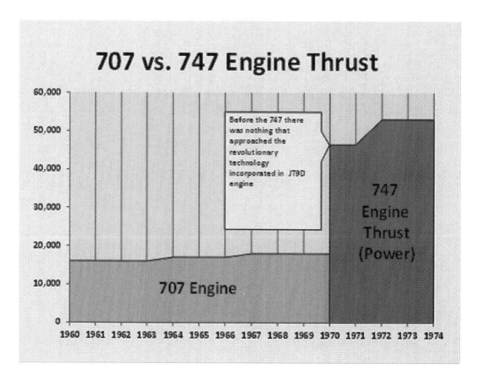

707 vs. 747 Engine Thrust

Before the 747 there was nothing that approached the revolutionary technology incorporated in JT9D engine

747 Engine Thrust (Power)

707 Engine

Typically, engine development leads aircraft development by at least a few years, but not with the 747. As Boeing's Joe Sutter wrote, "Never before in the history of commercial aviation had a new type of airliner been developed for a type of engine that didn't exist yet."

What was so astonishing about this new aircraft and engine technology was that none of it had any extensive operating time in the military, which had historically been in the forefront of airplane design. The first flight testing of the JT9D was done as a single-engine flying test bed on a B52 in June 1968. While the Boeing 707 had been a derivative of extensive military technology, the 747 was not a derivative of anything flying in the military. None of us in maintenance and engineering had ever seen anything like it before, or indeed since.

THE CHAOTIC INITIAL MANUFACTURING PROCESS

Boeing was facing an *incredible* challenge in the first year of production. In fact, the challenges for the design engineers were so great that Sutter's group was dubbed *"the incredibles."* They had scheduled and promised deliveries for approximately one hundred aircraft during the first year, and their design engineers and technicians were operating within a compressed time period and under considerable pressure to meet production deadlines. To make matters worse, business and financial pressures were weighing heavily on the management of both Boeing and Pratt & Whitney. Many historians have indicated that Boeing literally was betting the company on the 747. As Sutter wrote:

> *For the first time ever, a fundamentally new type of commercial airplane was being shaken out at the same time as a fundamentally new type of engine. I can't think of another time this has happened; in most cases, the engine is a year or two ahead of the airplane. The fates of Boeing and Pratt were firmly intertwined, because the failure of either company's ambitious development would have spelled disaster for the other.*

I spent the spring and summer of 1969 at the factory and each week I would a tour a few of our new staff around the factory and flight line. Our primary purpose for being at the factory was to become familiar with a real live airplane. It was important to physically locate those components and areas that would require routine servicing, and more generally to touch as much hardware as possible. The great challenge was that while you could review aircraft manuals and procedures, realistically it was essential to become very familiar with a completed aircraft. This became a major problem since there was not one completed aircraft until very late in the program.

Unlike other new aircraft programs, there was no prototype 747 until Boeing rolled out Aircraft RA 001 in October 1968. It was a grand media event with twenty-six airlines present, but the 747 was far from complete. No one other than Boeing personnel could get near the airplane. After that October rollout, the first test flight of RA 001 did not occur until February 9, 1969.

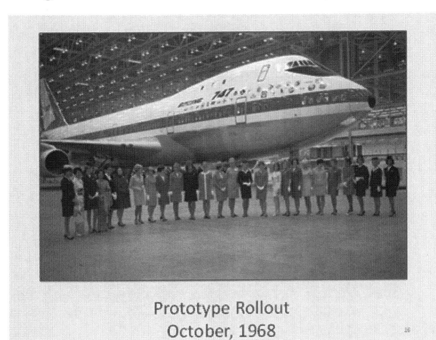

Prototype Rollout
October, 1968

What is important to remember about the first test flight is the date: February 9, 1969. Pan Am was to receive its first aircraft deliveries just ten months later, in late December 1969—an *incredibly* short time frame for developing and completing the flight test program for a high-tech aircraft. Joe Sutter candidly wrote, "If I could have changed any aspect of the 747 program, it would have been our schedule."

The first 747 flight was spectacular. What a thrill to see this gigantic flying machine lumber down the runway, majestically lift off of the ground—and actually fly! There had been many skeptics, so both the aviation world and the real world were closely watching. Boeing desperately wanted the flight to appear as just an everyday occurrence. Chief test pilot Jack Waddell said the aircraft handled like "a pilot's dream." On the surface and for public consumption it did appear as if everything was moving along on plan, but behind the scenes there were enormous obstacles. For example, Waddell was so concerned about the engines, as Joe Sutter later reported, that "the first flight had 40 automobile batteries hooked up to hydraulic pumps so in case he lost all four engines he'd have flight controls." This was certainly not a ringing endorsement for an engine at that stage of its development.

Sutter went on to note numerous complaints about the engines when flying the 747 to the Paris Air Show in June 1969:

> *By far the biggest challenge was getting four adequate engines. Almost every JT9D we got from Pratt & Whitney in those early days lacked the reliability and surge margins needed to allow our test fleet to depart the immediate vicinity of our test flight area.*

It didn't take long to determine that the engine problems were huge. None of the aircraft coming off the assembly line had engines. Hanging in place of the engines were concrete blocks to keep the weight distributed so that the aircraft could be moved. The Boeing and Pratt relationship and the success of the program, as Sutter wrote, were "very intertwined," but at this late stage of development their relationship, for many reasons, was souring.

First Test Flight
February 9, 1969

Other major components were also missing as the aircraft came off the assembly line. Some aircraft were missing the pylons from which the engine hung. Others had dollies in place of the landing gear. The Boeing flight line next to the plant was filled with incomplete 747 aircraft, which meant that work had to be tailored to individual aircraft and completed outside on the flight line, all of which was exceedingly labor intensive.

In hindsight, the reason for the manufacturing chaos was understandable. It takes a long lead time to build and assemble any airplane, no less a 747. Boeing began building and assembling the 747 long before the first prototype ever flew. This presented the company with an extremely unusual manufacturing scenario because as problems developed in the flight test program, those problems had to be corrected, redesigned, and fixes incorporated back into the aircraft on the assembly line. In retrospect, it was remarkable that Boeing could pull off this high-wire act at all. Joe Sutter said it best:

> *More than once I wondered what had possessed our management to commit to having a 747 completed in two thirds the amount of time it ordinarily takes to develop an all-new jet. —and— Pratt was in dire trouble developing the 747's engine.*

It had become very apparent, given the airplane's size, technology, and our factory experience, that the 747 was going to be a major task for the world's airlines to digest, under the best of circumstances. It would be especially difficult for Pan Am, which was receiving twenty-five aircraft in nine months. Unfortunately, the record will show that the 747 operation during the early years *never* occurred under the best of circumstances.

CERTIFICATION FLIGHT NIGHTMARE

We returned to New York's JFK in the early fall of 1969 to continue preparing for the aircraft deliveries beginning in December 1969. An essential milestone for both Pan Am and Boeing was the certification flight, the final step in obtaining the FAA's approval that the 747 aircraft and the airline were qualified to safely carry passengers. The certification flight is a full-blown dress rehearsal of a typical scheduled operation utilizing all the airline's maintenance, ground, and flight operations personnel. The flight was scheduled to operate from JFK to London carrying approximately three hundred company employees. On board would be numerous FAA inspectors observing every detail of the operation, both on the ground and in flight.

The certification aircraft was flown to JFK from Seattle by Pan Am pilots and arrived at the hangar about forty-eight hours prior to the December 30 departure. Since this was the first time we had a 747 at JFK under our full control, the passenger terminal personnel wanted the aircraft at the departure terminal to fit check some of their ground equipment. Assistant chief pilot Jess

Tranter, who flew the aircraft to JFK, checked some of us out on taxiing the aircraft from the hangar to the terminal.

When the aircraft was due to return to the hangar, I was taxiing. Joe Keegan, director of line service, was in the copilot's seat, and Don Day, manager of tech services, was in the flight engineer's seat. Off we went—just the three of us—totally alone on our first solo 747 taxi ride back to the hangar.

It was a heady experience steering an airplane from three stories up. All went well until we were a few hundred yards from the hangar. It was then our hangar ground crew reported we had black smoke coming from the number three engine. Looking down at the gauges, we noticed the engine had flamed out and the exhaust gas temperature was pegged in the red. We immediately shut down the engine fuel lever and discharged a fire bottle. Prior to the ground crew reporting smoke, we hadn't been looking at the engine gauges because the engines were only idling. Joe Keegan and I were obviously looking straight ahead to see where we were going, and Don Day was monitoring the flight engineer's panel, all of which was normal procedure.

We finished taxiing on three engines to the hangar ramp. When we inspected the engine that had flamed out, we found pieces of molten metal lying at the bottom of the exhaust tail pipe. The rear turbine blades were badly overheated. The engine had to be changed! It was a sickening feeling—our worst nightmare occurring on the FAA certification aircraft, no less.

We had a spare engine, but we hadn't practiced much with the new engine change equipment. Realistically, no one expected to use the engine change equipment for many months into the operation. We had decided for many reasons to use different lift equipment for the engine change and a totally different approach than Boeing's. So here we were with another first—swinging a five-ton engine from a forklift, using new access stands, working many feet off of the ground. It was staggering that all this was happening only about six hours after the certification aircraft had arrived at JFK.

Given the history of engine development problems, it was noticeably strange that there was not one word, absolutely nothing, about the engine problem from either the Pratt or Boeing representatives assigned to Pan Am. Everyone was so deeply mired in the effort to change the first engine that no one gave much thought to the cause of the flameout. At that point it was being treated as a random event. A sea of mechanics, supervisors, and service engineers was blanketing the engine change. The word "circus" comes to mind.

Miraculously, our people completed the engine change in time for an engine test run, and we did taxi the aircraft to the terminal for an on-time departure. The certification flight to London was successful, and both Pan Am and Boeing received FAA certification approval on December 31, 1969. It was a significant milestone in the history of commercial aviation.

An Embarrassing Inaugural

The next much-anticipated flight would be the inaugural of the first B747 commercial service—a major historic event for Pan Am, Boeing, and commercial aviation. The flight, JFK to London, was scheduled for early evening on January 21, 1970. This indeed would be the Main Event.

Before the flight we met with the cockpit crew: Pan Am chief pilot Bob Weeks, copilot Jess Tranter, and flight engineer Bernie Reilly. The purpose of the meeting was to brief and caution them about our experience with the certification aircraft. While taxiing with the engines simply at idle, an engine had flamed out, causing a tail-pipe fire. The crew never said anything, but our sense was they might have assumed that maintenance had done something wrong, which at that time was probably not an unreasonable assumption.

About twelve hours prior to the inaugural flight, our second aircraft arrived at JFK. Pan Am's chief factory representative, Bob Blake, had been pressing Boeing hard for the second aircraft so it would be at JFK in time to be used as a cover (backup) aircraft if required.

The inaugural aircraft was at the departure terminal early to allow plenty of time for loading and provisioning. It was an enormous media event. The flight was loaded with dignitaries, reporters, high-level executives from many vendors including Boeing and Pratt & Whitney, television talk show host David Susskind, and many celebrities, including Charles Lindbergh who stayed clear of the media and TV cameras. It was not your typical passenger manifest. Electricity filled the air in this incredibly festive atmosphere. As Jerry Spampanato, our director of passenger service, noted:

> *Since Pan Am was the first carrier to introduce the 747 there was a natural curiosity from the other airlines and airport employees. On the day of the inaugural flight there was a large assembly of airport employees on the tarmac observing the loading and ground handling of the flight. In fact the Port Authority Police and operations staff were called upon to control the crowds of airport employees.*

The aircraft departed the gate a little late due to a loading delay. After the engines were running and the aircraft had taxied away from the terminal, many of us went to the Clipper Club on the second floor of the terminal to watch and toast the takeoff. It was now dark, very windy and cold, with a few snow flurries, but we could clearly see the biggest airplane on the airport. The taillights on the Pan Am logo and rotating beacon were very visible.

Suddenly the 747 turned around. It looked like it was heading back to the terminal. The control center notified us that the aircraft had a problem—an engine problem. We ran down to stop the aircraft before it reached the gate. We plugged in a ground headset to talk with the flight crew. The flight engineer Bernie Reilly said very loudly, "The number four engine has flamed out and the EGT [exhaust gas temperature] is pegged in the red!" The aircraft was brought back to the gate for inspection. As expected, there were pieces of molten metal lying at the bottom of the exhaust tail pipe, and the rear turbine blades were badly overheated. The engine had to be changed—another worst nightmare!

We returned to the hangar to get the cover aircraft ready. The passenger terminal was in a state of turmoil. The poor passenger service people, who were now in a total state of shock, had to deal with the passengers, the media, and a host of other logistical and emotional issues as Spampanato describes below. And of course the world was watching.

> *The passengers had to disembark and were taken by buses to an off airport restaurant for dinner. An aircraft swap was made with a second new 747 that was renamed Clipper America. Under normal circumstances loading the original aircraft for the first time was a challenge. Now the cargo and galley loads had to be transferred from one aircraft to the other, and the Worldport departure terminal was still under construction which made the load transfer more difficult and challenging, to say the least.*

When we arrived at the hangar, the tug was hooked up to the cover aircraft and the painters were just finishing stenciling the name of the original departure aircraft, *Clipper Young America*, on the side of the aircraft. I do not recall whose idea that was, and none of us gave it much thought at the time, although in retrospect it seems to have captured the interest of many people.

By the time we started taxiing the cover aircraft back to the terminal, the wind was picking up. It was cold and gusty. Having had the experience of two engines failing while simply idling, everyone was totally focused on watching for a flameout. Don Day, who was at the flight engineer's panel, moved his seat forward to watch the engine gauges closely on the pilot's instrument panel.

If an engine started to spool down (flame out), he would shut off the fuel lever immediately, preventing fuel from pouring into a stalled engine and causing another exhaust tail-pipe fire. This actually became the procedure the flight crews would use until the problem was corrected. Thankfully we did not experience any problems on the taxi back to the terminal, but there were many eyes watching from the terminal as the aircraft taxied on to the gate.

When the passengers started to reboard, Waguih Ouess, our passenger service supervisor, was at the gate, "reassuring passengers that the flight will be great, while demonstrators were outside the Terminal comparing the 747 to the *Titanic!*" After an exhausting and emotional experience for everyone associated with our inaugural flight, the world's first scheduled commercial 747 flight finally departed—six hours late.

Detail from painting by John T. McCoy showing Clipper Young America's arrival at London Heathrow Airport 22 January 1970. Captain Robert M. Weeks and

crew flew the Pan American World Airways Boeing 747-121, N736PA New York to London on a 6 hour, 43 minute inaugural passenger-carrying flight of the new wide-body jet. Aboard were a crew of 20 and 335 passengers.

A *New York Times* reporter on the flight wrote an article, "Substitute 747 Off for London; Engine Trouble Causes Delay" (a fascinating read) in which he quoted Captain Weeks, who was probably putting the best face on the situation, as saying, "Due to gusty winds we were getting no flow of air from the front to the back in the engine. It is like someone put a cover on the top of your chimney and battened your furnace up." In the same article the reporter wrote:

> *Representatives of United Aircraft, the parent company of Pratt & Whitney which makes the 747's giant engines, gave a somewhat different explanation of what they called a 'serious deficiency' that they planned to remedy as quickly as possible. The manufacturer said that crosswinds had blocked the engine's air intake, causing a condition equivalent to the flooding of a car engine. The fuel however continued to burn causing a compressor stall.*

It seemed surreal that Pratt & Whitney would admit a "serious deficiency" that they planned to "remedy as quickly as possible." Obviously Pratt knew the engine had a tendency to stall at idle speed, especially in windy, crosswind conditions, and they were working on a fix. If they had only shared this information with us, the trauma and expense of the certification and inaugural flights could have been avoided.

Another interesting take on all of this was the passenger reaction. You have the captain giving a somewhat odd explanation to the passengers about the engine problem, and the engine manufacturer reporting the engine has a "serious deficiency." Couple that with the fact that the inaugural aircraft was the only flyable 747 in the world, yet all the passengers simply reboarded, without any trepidation, and flew off over the Atlantic to London. In the context of today's world, the calm passenger reaction to the delay was clearly unusual. Sort of an undying faith the passengers had in the integrity of a company, in this case Pan American. Surprisingly, the *Times* article didn't prompt any further investigation into the matter, and media coverage regarding the aircraft's reliability problems was almost nonexistent.

STRUGGLING MIGHTILY
WITH POOR RELIABILITY

This new technology engine was clearly the 747's Achilles' heel in the early years. In retrospect the JT9D's poor initial reliability was understandable given the milestone dates of its development.

Consider that one test JT9 engine (i.e. a single engine) strapped to an experimental air force B52 bomber flew for the very first time in June 1968. That's only eight months prior to the 747 prototype's first flight in February 1969. And remember on that flight the chief test pilot had batteries installed for the hydraulic system in case they lost all four engines. As previously noted, Boeing had difficulty finding four good engines for the Paris Air Show in June 1969. And our two most important first flights, the certification flight in December 1969 and the inaugural flight in January 1970, each had an engine failure before the aircraft ever left the ground. What follows is only the tip of the iceberg of a long, complex list of maintenance and operational issues.

Early on, the engine was plagued with a number of flight safety problems, such as stalling, flameouts, oil loss, and first-stage turbine failures, many of which resulted in an in-flight shutdown. One of the more serious events was a first-stage turbine blade failure, which often occurred at a crucial time such as takeoff or in the early stages of climb. This type of failure caused nerve-rattling compressor stalls, which were heard and felt by the passengers and crew. Such an incident almost always resulted in dumping excess fuel and returning to the departure airport.

Pilots are well trained to handle an engine failure, but realistically when one of these monster engines stalls with a loud *bang* just as the aircraft leaves the ground, especially at night or in heavy weather, it takes steady pilot skills to cope with the situation. In fact, pilots use an abnormal procedure checklist for the engine shutdown, dumping fuel, and making a three-engine landing—although "abnormal" might be a slight oversimplification.

During an air turn back, the cabin crew is also confronted with an abnormal operation. They have to hurriedly stow equipment to prepare the cabin for landing and cope with concerns and questions from the passengers, all while trying to maintain a routine, business-as-usual demeanor. Once back on the ground, the passenger service staff challenges are enormous, especially at the outlying stations. To put the magnitude of this type of problem in perspective, an in-flight engine failure during takeoff rarely happens today. If it did, the event would be front-page news. Our airline alone experienced dozens of such events each year.

And there were also unscheduled engine changes that occurred as a result simply of a pilot discrepancy report. In that regard, Pan Am, TWA, and many international airlines had a cadre of experienced flight engineers who were qualified on the 707 and 747 from the beginning. These engineers were technically sharp, had that sixth sense for detecting system problems. One of them, Jack Grimshaw, who at ninety-three is still technically sharp, developed and championed an effective in-flight engine monitoring system that often detected incipient engine problems before an in-flight catastrophic failure occurred.

Flight engineers like the Grimshaws of the world made an enormous contribution in those early years of the 747. Ironically, the bittersweet aspect of their contribution was that the 747 would be the flight engineers' swan song. Later-model 747s utilized sophisticated, efficient, computerized systems for monitoring not only the engine, but all aircraft systems. This resulted in streamlining the cockpit for two pilots, instead of two pilots and a flight engineer by eliminating the flight engineer's panel on the right side of the cockpit shown below. A truly marvelous technical advancement, although the cockpit environment has probably become a little less—interesting:

There were also dozens and dozens of unscheduled engine removals because of problems found during maintenance inspections. Consequently, there were often aircraft grounded awaiting engines. Many engine changes had to be accomplished outside in terrible weather—an extraordinary, unforgettable hardship for the mechanics and supervisors. As Jim Smeriglio, Pan Am maintenance supervisor, noted, "It was amazing that in time we could replace an engine in under three hours. But it was discouraging to see these gliders parked on the ramp." Gene Scime, a maintenance supervisor with a sharp crew of engine mechanics, noted:

We did so many engine changes and got so good at it, that the supervisors and mechanics started to try and beat each other on the quickest time with a fully QEC engine. It not only gave the crews a sense of pride but helped the Airline keep going without a major engine change delay. I remember a cargo aircraft just had an air turn back with an engine failure and would be at the hanger spot 4 shortly. We set up two fork lifts. One with an engine ready to go and an empty one to remove the failed engine. By the time the crew got off the aircraft we had the engine off and away from the aircraft. The captain told me he was going to eat with the crew and I told him to make it a quick sandwich, you'll be ready to go shortly. I think we took 2 hours and 40 minutes. It made the company Newsletter the next day.

Although the aircraft service crews became proficient in replacing engines, the more significant problem was repairing the removed engines. The engine repair and overhaul workload had become overwhelming. Pan Am and all of the major 747 operators had large engine repair facilities, but it takes time to tear down the engine, route and repair the defective parts, collect the material, and rebuild the engine. Repairing an extensively damaged engine is extraordinarily complex, and the material costs are astronomical. Even in those days the cost of a single engine repair could exceed a million dollars. Boeing was not immune to engine shortages either, as indicated by this photo, showing nineteen 747s parked awaiting engines.

Everett Flight Line
1970

Another costly issue was shipping engines to and from stations throughout the world. The JT9D engine was too large to fit in the cargo compartment of a passenger 747, so for many years the engine had to be shipped utilizing the fifth-pod method. The fifth pod was a full-size engine installed and fitted within a unique "fifth-pod kit" and attached to the underside of the wing as noted below. It was not a simple process to build a five-ton engine into a fifth-pod configuration and attach it to the wing of the delivering aircraft. It's easy to imagine there were often interesting comments by some of the passengers and crew when they saw the fifth-pod configuration while boarding the aircraft.

Apart from the engine the initial operating reliability of systems such as electrical, flight control, landing gear, and instrumentation caused delays and incidents, but they were not as dramatic, or as costly as the engine. They were difficult problems nonetheless. The trailing-edge flaps, tires, and brakes were high-maintenance items. A number of serious incidents occurred on heavy-gross-weight takeoffs because of brake overheating. During taxiing the high temperature from the brake would cause a tire to go flat. On takeoff the flat tire would disintegrate and shed its tread. When the gear was raised, the shredded rubber from the tire would often damage the aircraft structure or rupture hydraulic lines. The list of aircraft system problems is long, varied and too complex to enumerate, but there are documents in the Appendix which specifically identify some of the problems.

Reliability problems of this nature result in the pilots having to manage a high rate of non-routine in-flight situations. In effect, the book on abnormal in-flight events was being written as the operation moved forward. Paul Roitsch, Pan Ams technical chief pilot has an interesting note in the section, The Borger Files, on coping with abnormal in-flight incidents. Needless to say these events require a high degree of flight crew proficiency. Yet remember, this was an era when there were no 747 flight simulators and pilots had to acquire their skills solely by live flying. It was extraordinary to see a 747 jumbo aircraft performing landings and takeoffs (touch and go's) like a little Piper or Cessna aircraft in flight training. Engine failures were simulated by pulling a throttle back to idle. The training maneuvers were fascinating to watch if you had the good fortune to be a cockpit observer. The challenges and experiences of the early pilot training would be, in themselves, a remarkable story.

It's important to emphasize the problems that have been described thus far are not simply a few dramatic, isolated incidents, but rather capture the overall operating tenor of the fleet. The Borger Files will further substantiate and quantify the length and breadth of the 747's early reliability history.

THE BORGER FILES

John Borger joined Pan American World Airways in January 1935 shortly after graduating from the Massachusetts Institute of Technology, where he received a BS degree in aeronautical engineering. His Pan Am career of forty-seven years covered a wide range of engineering achievements from the early Clippers, Constellations, DC-6, DC-7, Boeing 707, the Falcon, Concorde, the US SST, and the 747. He was an industry icon and a member of numerous prestigious aeronautical and engineering industry societies. As Pan Am's chief engineer, Borger was Juan Trippe's point man on everything technical, and he had a significant influence during the early stages of the 747 design.

"Borge" was a large man with an intimidating presence. When Borger spoke, Boeing listened. Yet despite that commanding presence, he was a kind, considerate gentleman. He and Joe Sutter had a mutually respectful relationship dating back to the B377 and B707. Sutter writes:

> *Borger's fingers were all over the aircraft. A good friend and living legend in aviation, John Borger was a rock-solid technical expert. He did his job full tilt and was*

unsparing of those who didn't give him definitive answers to his probing questions.

Later in life, while Borger was living with his daughter in Pennsylvania, he received an invitation to a Wings Club luncheon in New York, where Joe Sutter was the featured speaker. Borger desperately wanted to see his old friend again, so Boeing hosted a private brunch for Sutter, Borger, and few close friends, including Niels Anderson, a project engineer who had worked for Borger. At the brunch Borger's daughter asked Anderson if he had any interest in a room full of boxes filled with her father's personal files.

It was a stroke of good fortune that Anderson quickly accepted the invitation. When he visited Borger, he found him as sharp as ever. They discussed cataloging the files, which Anderson eventually did over a period of five days. Niels Anderson's effort preserved approximately sixteen large file boxes of documents. Ultimately, through the Pan Am Historical Foundation, the files were forwarded to the Richter Library at the University of Miami and added to the large Pan Am Collection.

The 747 portion of the Borger Files contains revealing correspondence and specific data that buttress the eyewitness accounts discussed thus far. The files are a vital confirmation of the enormous struggles the airlines had coping with the 747's poor reliability. Because many of these documents are highly technical, we've included in the appendixes only those that support our comments and analysis. The appendix page number is shown in parentheses **(A 00)** where applicable.

The files clearly indicate, from the beginning of the 747's inaugural flight in January 1970 through the heavy summer flying months in 1970 and 1971, the 747 had considerable reliability problems. The reliability and performance of the JT9D was especially abysmal. In a letter to the division president of Pratt & Whitney dated Aug 20, 1970 detailing the problems, Borger closes with:

> *We know your people are working on fixes, but we badly need a more specific and accelerated 'get well' program. The 747 is making a poor reputation for scheduled reliability. We hope that you will join us in our effort to improve reliability for the fall and winter season.* **(A: 1, 2).** There was very little improvement in summer 1971 **(A: 20).**

For the first 16 months of the 747 operation, the industry operating reliability and in-flight incidents were of such a concern that a high level industry meeting hosted by Pan Am was held in the Pan Am Building on April 28, 1971. In attendance were flight operations, maintenance and engineering executives from all of the North American airlines operating the 747, high level executives from Boeing, (including Joe Sutter), Pratt & Whitney and the FAA **(A: 3, 4).**

The outline for the meeting was a Boeing and Pratt & Whitney talking points document covering a long list of problems. The document candidly highlighted the major engine problems and a list of significant aircraft system problems and planned corrective actions. While Pan Am was the dominant 747 carrier, the document addressed the problems and statistics for the entire industry **(A: 5, 6).**

It's an illuminating presentation that specifically details the serious in-flight engine problems during the 747's first 16 months of operation **(A: 7, 8).** The sheer number of unscheduled engine removals and in-flight shutdowns was staggering, even for 1970's technology. The high engine removal and shutdown rates per 1000 engine hours (a standard industry measurement) for such an extended period of time had never been seen in the industry before or since **(A: 19, 20).** All of this commentary on the engine performance is confirmed by the following excerpts from the meeting:

> *To date the 747 has experienced approximately 431 engine inflight shutdowns.*
>
> *The two major causes were 1) loss of lubrication oil pressure and or quantity and 2) engine stall and over temperature. The rate peaked at 5.7 shutdowns per 1000 hours in early June.*
>
> *There have been 5 cases of multiple power loss in flight [i.e. two engines were shut down for a period of time], one of which resulted in a 2 engine out landing.*
>
> *25 in flight power plant fires – January 1970 – April 1971* **(A: 8).**

Apart from the engine there were many significant aircraft system problems on the agenda, with special attention to the trailing-edge flaps, which was an excessively high-maintenance system. The document noted that Boeing planned thirteen modifications and manufacturing changes to the trailing-edge flap system. Based on the document's table of contents, it's clear that they had a lively discussion. Nonetheless, the meeting concluded with cocktails and dinner **(A: 9).**

Most of these reliability issues adversely affected in-flight operations, pilot procedures, and cockpit workload. Simply looking at the number of engine removals doesn't tell the true story of the cockpit workload leading up to an engine removal. For instance, prior to the removal of an engine for high EGT temperature, the engine might have required close monitoring on takeoff for a number of flight legs to keep the engine from over temping.

Pan Am's technical chief pilot Paul Roitsch wrote a revealing six page letter to a base chief pilot detailing cockpit procedures utilized to cope with many of the problems discussed in the April 1971 industry meeting. Although the letter is written in a matter-of-fact manner, many of the problems he describes are serious engine and aircraft system problems which resulted in abnormal in-flight events. An especially critical engine problem was that the early aircraft, at high altitude were prone to stalling and flaming out when the throttles were rapidly reduced. When the aircraft was over 35,000 feet a throttle bar was put in place so that the pilots would not rapidly decelerate the engine. The following are also a few interesting quotes on aircraft system problems:

> *At random, brakes would release at low taxi speeds causing collision hazard.*
> *Start of takeoff several pilots' experienced severe directional excursions.*
> *Concern about the possibility of body gear steering unlocking at high speed causing an undesired lateral translation.*
> *On at least two occasions segments of trailing edge flaps left the aircraft in flight.*

For anyone interested in pursuing more of the technical details, the letter: "Résumé of B747 Introduction Problems and Operational Solutions" is in the Appendix and speaks for itself **(A: 10-15)**.

It was *incredible* when you think of what the flight crews had to contend with then, compared with today. And it wasn't the result of 1970s technology, because the reliability of the 707 at that time was superb, compared to the 747.

While all levels of flight operations, maintenance, and engineering throughout the world were struggling with the day-to-day operation, the Pan Am legal department was preparing a document titled "Excessive Boeing 747 Costs." The opening paragraph of the document, dated June 29, 1970, noted:

The unusual problems encountered with the 747s (including the JT9D engine) have resulted in heavy excess costs, which are continuing. It is important that these be identified, related to specific causes and measured, in order to support claims for damage for breach of contract. **(A: 16)**

It's apparent from the files that given the aircraft's performance, there had been a number of discussions relative to guarantees and liability claims with both Boeing and United Aircraft (Pratt & Whitney). This exchange continued over a long period of time. Finally in March 1972, a draft was prepared for Chairman Seawell to the chairmen of the boards for Boeing and United Aircraft (Pratt & Whitney), which began:

As I know you have been aware for some time, Pan Am's experience with the 747 aircraft and the JT9D engine has been quite disappointing in many respects. You will recall that at the time of initial delivery of the first aircraft in December 1969 it was recognized that the aircraft failed to comply with certain of the more important performance guarantees of the contract. These problems were to have been resolved completely by March 1971; but they have not been, and it is perfectly clear that there is no prospect in the near future that they will be.

The aircraft's engines, of course, have been a source of extreme concern right from the beginning. **(A: 17)**

The draft concluded with a formal claim for reimbursement of *$21.6 million* in a "Schedule of Damages Thru March 1972" **(A: 18)**.

Before concluding the Borger Files comments, just a few words about the man himself shown below. Borge was the center point of contact for the chairman and top-level corporate officers for all operational and technical aspects of the airline. This included new aircraft specifications, and interfacing with the major vendors and the operating departments within the company. High on his list of responsibilities were the almost constant design changes to the interior configurations. In addition to the technical challenges of the early 747s, the working environment at that time in the corporate headquarters was difficult—to say the least. There was a constant churning in the corporate organization both in structure and people.

Through all of this aircraft reliability and corporate management turmoil, Borge was a steady, stabilizing influence for flight operations, maintenance, and engineering. I had the great privilege of getting to know Borge well both professionally and personally. He had great wisdom, was tough, and never complained. He was in a position to possess extremely sensitive information, which he scrupulously kept confidential. Despite his iconic industry status, he did not take himself very seriously. It's difficult to imagine the 747's early years without John Borger.

Too Many Airplanes

Another point often overlooked is that the reliability and performance issues were greatly exacerbated by the fleet's size, which was astonishing. Boeing delivered almost one hundred airplanes in the first year of production. Never again did they come close to delivering that many 747s. This was a significant challenge for those airlines with large fleets, like Pan Am, TWA, British Airways, and JAL. Actually, Pan Am took delivery of twenty-five aircraft in the first year and eight more the second year. Total aircraft deliveries in the first two years accounted for approximately 70 percent of all 747s delivered in the first five years of the operation as seen in the following chart:

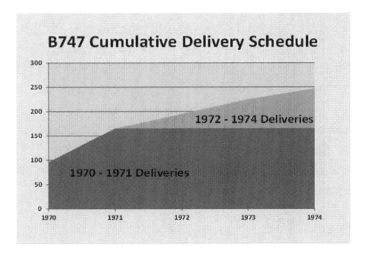

Rapid fleet growth, coupled with problems which were endemic throughout the airline world, greatly complicated the maintenance and modification process because there were many airplanes and engines with all of the same problems. And since the JT9D was the only engine on the early 747s, given the engine issues, the material demand pressures on Pratt & Whitney and other engine vendors was enormous. You could not call with a purchase order for three sets of turbine blades and expect to get them anytime soon. The same was true for Boeing with material required for chronic aircraft system problems. There is a common acronym "AOG" utilized in the airline material and supply departments. It means "aircraft on ground." This was an era of AOGs.

The good news with a large fleet build up was, although it was extremely painful for the airlines, in a short period of time the fleet amassed thousands of flight hours and maintenance service experience, which greatly contributed to the analysis of reliability data. Input from the early operating experience was crucial, providing Boeing and Pratt with valuable data to incorporate improvements.

But the bad news was these were not simply improvements of maintenance procedures and inspections, but rather the requirement to install newly designed hardware and components. Not a happy prospect for the airlines modifying essentially brand new, recently delivered airplanes, nor easy to accomplish especially on the internal sections of the engine. Because of the rapid fleet growth in the first two years of the operation it was a gargantuan task to "get well" quickly.

When reflecting on this early history it's essential to keep in mind that, collectively, all of the following major aspects that have been discussed thus far loomed large and greatly affected the airline's performance during the introduction of the 747:

Major Service Introduction Challenges

Revolutionary Technology → Size → Poor Reliability → The Fleet Size Yrs 1 & 2

KEEPING THE PROGRAM FROM UNRAVELING

The numerous eyewitness reports and the Borger Files convincingly demonstrate the 747's reliability in the early years was a major concern not only at Pan Am, but also throughout the industry. The situation persisted for a long period of time as confirmed by the industry meeting on significant reliability issues that was mentioned above, which was held in April 1971, sixteen months into the operation.

As discussed in the beginning, all of this history thus far is totally contrary to the *Wikipedia* description of the 747's service introduction where they note that *"Although technical problems occurred, they were relatively minor and quickly solved."* The facts indicate that a more accurate characterization of the 747's introduction experience is:

From the inception of the commercial aviation jet age, there has never been a period of time similar to the early operation of the 747, which was plagued by serious in-flight incidents, overwhelmingly poor engine reliability, and numerous mechanical

aircraft system problems. The schedule disruptions and costs associated with these reliability issues were huge.

Finally, in view of this sobering history, we're left with an obvious question. Just how was it possible for the 747 to fly through this turbulent period to become the reliable, superb aircraft of today? From a historical perspective it's a fair question to ponder and debate. A good starting point to begin such a discussion might be to consider there were probably three major factors that kept the 747 flying safely during this period.

First, Boeing's original basic design has clearly stood the test of time. The overall fuselage length and wing span did not change, even in the 747-300 which entered service in early 1980 and is still in service today. As shown below, except for an enlarged extended upper deck and more windows, the 747-100 and -300 in exterior appearance are almost identical:

Overall Length = 231 ft 10 in
Wing Span = 195 ft 8 in
Tail Height = 63 ft 5 in
Cabin Width = 20

747-100

Overall Length - 231 ft 10 in
Wing Span - 195 ft 8 in
Tail Height - 63 ft 5 in
Cabin Width - 20

747-300

The Boeing design philosophy on system redundancy to ensure the safety of the primary systems like the flight controls and landing gear was exceptional. The primary flight control systems were excellent. As chief test pilot Jack Waddell noted on the747's first flight, it was a "pilot's dream." The pilots loved the handling characteristics of the airplane. Boeing knew early on that these systems would perform under the most adverse circumstances because of a major incident that occurred on Pan Am Flight 845 from San Francisco to Tokyo in 1971.

As a result of using incorrect takeoff performance calculations, the aircraft ran out of runway on takeoff and barely managed to become airborne. During liftoff, the tail section structure was severely damaged and the rear cabin floor buckled, seriously injuring three passengers. A few unoccupied seats were destroyed. The aircraft lost three of its four hydraulic systems, drastically degrading many of the aircraft operating systems, especially the flight control system.

The flight crew managed to stabilize the aircraft and return to the airport. During the landing and before coming to a stop, the 747 settled on its tail because the body landing gear was unlocked, which resulted in the evacuation slides failing to touch the ground. The cabin crew miraculously evacuated the aircraft safely. This was the mother of all worst-case flight-test scenarios—and the 747 passed with flying colors.

**Pan Am Flight 845 SFO to TYO
February, 1971** 27

Certainly at that point in 1971, and probably since, no other 747 aircraft had ever flown in a configuration where the primary flight control and hydraulic systems had been so severely degraded. In addition, the tail section's horizontal stabilizer and the underside of the rear fuselage had been badly damaged. Flight 845 was a real live confirmation of the integrity and strength of Boeing's flight control, landing gear, and tail structure design. Interestingly, the tail number of Flight 845 was N747!

Second, there was a functional industry alliance, which included the airlines, manufacturers, and the FAA, that worked together to address flight safety and reliability problems. The high-level industry meeting of April 1971, as noted in the Borger Files, was a typical example of this type of collaborative effort. Even today nothing meaningful can be changed in the aircraft's flight-operating and maintenance procedures unless there is agreement within this alliance. Despite their many technical differences of opinion, everyone during that era genuinely wanted to make the 747 a success. Their primary objective was to work among themselves to reach a consensus for action on difficult flight safety and maintenance problems.

The alliance would address serious incidents by immediately implementing an action to ensure the aircraft's safety. They would then take intermediate remedial action and develop a program for the final fix. Since the 747 problems were multifaceted, this corrective action process was the practical alternative to not grounding the airplane. During this tumultuous time, there was enormous pressure on Boeing and Pratt & Whitney, and both companies worked feverishly to develop massive maintenance and modification "get well" programs.

As an aside, for many of us involved with the early 747s, it was hard to fathom that with twenty-first-century technology, the 787 was grounded for five months for a single issue: a battery. The 787's grounding was in fact the longest in aviation history. To put this in perspective, that's almost 20 percent of the time it took to build the 747 from start to finish. By comparison, the industry's collaborative effort kept the 747 operation from an unraveling fate like the 787's. And it was not simply good luck. The 747's safety record is proof positive that the industry alliance's process was hugely successful.

Third, and most important, the day-to-day performance of the people on the front lines of flight operations and maintenance was truly *incredible*, which in today's world might sound a little trite. This was a time when there were no computer programs or algorithms to provide answers for problems. Critical decisions were made by people, based only on their training, a hard-copy manual (many inches thick, with no Google references), and their experience. Remember, this was the "new technology" airplane with a myriad of serious problems operating at a time when technical support was, in effect, rudimentary. It was an operating world that was far from routine. Flight crews and maintenance were constantly faced with making *go* or *no-go* decisions. Given our current digital world, this might not sound extraordinary, but it definitely was because it posed an enormous set of challenges that is difficult to envision today.

An interesting intangible worth noting is that the 747 itself seemed to be a great motivator. People wanted to be identified with the aircraft. Airport ground staff, maintenance supervisors, and mechanics would stay around after their shift was finished just to follow up on problems. The list of colleagues who did this is extensive. These were not high-salaried employees who received special recognition but simply selfless contributors to a team effort. During that unique time in aviation history, there were many of these selfless contributors in other departments and other airlines. The 747 seemed to bring out the very best in people at a crucial time in aviation history when the very best was necessary.

And finally, our hope is that this narrative has told at least some of the untold story of the overwhelming operational challenges the airlines faced during the 747's early years. Clearly, there is more to tell. But for now, the thousands of airline people throughout the world who participated in this historic event should reflect with great pride on their enormous contribution in safely launching the Queen of the Sky.

THE AUTHOR

Ron Marasco began his career with Pan Am in 1956 as a Flight Engineer. He later transferred to maintenance and engineering and a few years before the 747 entered service was appointed General Manager of 747 Maintenance. From the beginning of the 747 operation until 1984 he held senior positions associated with all phases of 747 maintenance, including Vice President of Maintenance and Engineering. Subsequent to Pan Am he continued his 747 involvement as Senior Vice President of Operations for Flying Tigers, Atlas and Polar airlines, all of whom had large 747 cargo fleets. He was responsible for the operational start-up and obtaining the FAA Operating Certificate for Atlas and Polar airlines. In 1989 he received the coveted Air Transportation Association's *"Nuts and Bolts"* award, in recognition of outstanding professional leadership and management skills in airline maintenance and engineering for three decades and in celebration of his pioneering work in introducing the first and largest jumbo jet, the B747, into commercial service. He is currently on the Board of Directors of the Pan Am Historical Foundation and he and his wife Barbara live in East Hampton, New York. Visit Facebook on www.facebook.com/747tumultuousbeginning

APPENDIX

Note: For referencing purposes, the Borger file Appendix consists of twenty scanned pages from the Borger files in the Richter Library at the University of Miami. The following page numbers, 1 through 20, are referenced in the Section, The Borger Files, and are separate from the book's page numbering.

August 5, 1970

Mr. Bernard Schmickrath
Division President
Pratt & Whitney Aircraft
400 Main Street
East Hartford, Connecticut 06108

Dear Barney:

As you are most likely aware, the B747 on time departure record due to mechanical/maintenance problems has been a great disappointment. During July, 25.4% of the departures were delayed 15 minutes or more, with the basic engine (not including QEC) responsible for 19.3% of the total delays, (4.9% of departures). These compare to an overall rate of about 3% for the 707-321B. Engine problems have contributed to other delays, and many engine delays have been three – four hours.

Listed below, are the major engine items and the number of times the item contributed to a delay.

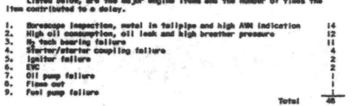

1.	Borescope inspection, metal in tailpipe and high AVM indication	14
2.	High oil consumption, oil leak and high breather pressure	12
3.	N_2 tach bearing failure	11
4.	Starter/starter coupling failure	4
5.	Ignitor failure	2
6.	EVC	2
7.	Oil pump failure	1
8.	Flame out	1
9.	Fuel pump failure	1
	Total	48

Obviously, the top of the list shows the items of major concern. With the high turbine module program drawing to a close, the first item should reduce. But we do not have similar fix programs for the other items, some of which have been with us since start of operations. Of major concern now are:

1. N_2 Tachometer Bearing
2. Variable stator vanes and control
3. Engine stall and overtemp
4. High EGT and overshoot
5. High oil consumption

1

Mr. Bernard Schmickrath   -2-   August 5, 1970

We know your people are working on fixes, but we badly need a more specific and accelerated "get well" program. The 747 is making a poor reputation for schedule reliability. We hope that you will join us in our effort to improve reliability for the Fall and Winter season.

Very truly yours,

J. G. Borger
Chief Engineer

2

Pan Am Building

April 28, 1971

AIR CANADA

J. W. Norberg - Vice President Maintenance
Capt. Benson - Director Flight Standards
Gordon Thoms - Director Line Maintenance

AMERICAN AIRLINES

BRANIFF

~ ～ . E. R. Bossange - Senior Vice President Engineering and Maintenance
H. Rumsey - Vice President - Flight Operations

CONTINENTAL AIR LINES

R. Steuben - Vice President - Flight Training
M. L. Taylor - Vice President - Engineering and Maintenance

DELTA AIR LINES

D. Hettermann - Asst. Vice President Engineering
T. P. Ball - Vice President Flight Operations
(D. B. Barclay)

EASTERN AIR LINES

Capt. P. Slayden - Technical Pilot
Col. W. Calhoun - Area Director - Maintenance
R. L. Moore - Vice President Maintenance (Possible)

NATIONAL AIRLINES

Capt. Royal
W. Schuling - Vice President Maintenance and Engineering

Continued.......

3

NORTHWEST AIRLINES

F. Judd - Vice President Maintenance and Engineering

PAN AMERICAN

T. Flanagan - Senior Vice President Operations
J. Weesner - Vice President Maintenance
J. Borger - Vice President and Chief Engineer

TRANS WORLD AIRLINES

E. Frankum - Vice President Flight Operations
G. Granger - Senior Director Flight Operations
C. Fisher - Maintenance Engineer
Mr. Roach - Maintenance Engineer

UNITED AIRLINES

H. Mays - Vice President Flight Operations
R. Collins - Vice President Engineering

BOEING

G. Nible - Vice President Customer Support
J. Sutter - General Manager - Everett Division
E. Pfaffman - Director Engineering - Everett Division
E. Webb

PRATT & WHITNEY

R. W. Baseler - Vice President Engineering
R. Hoff - Manager Product Support Engineering
G. Woodger - JT9D Project Engineer
R. Adams - Asst. to the President - Customer Liasion

FAA

R. Sliff - Deputy Director Flight Standards Service

ATA

E. Thomas - Director of Engineering

4

Appendix

D6-13050-920

747 TECHNICAL REVIEW MEETING
APRIL 28, 1971   PAN AM BUILDING, NEW YORK

5

TABLE OF CONTENTS

6

INFLIGHT ENGINE SHUTDOWN/FLAMEOUT

TO DATE THE 747 HAS EXPERIENCED APPROXIMATELY 431 ENGINE INFLIGHT SHUTDOWNS INCLUDING TRAINING AND FERRY FLIGHTS. A BREAKDOWN OF THE CAUSES FOR THESE SHUTDOWNS IS PRESENTED. THE TWO MAJOR CAUSES FOR SHUTDOWNS WERE (1) LOSS OF LUBRICATION OIL PRESSURE AND/OR QUANTITY AND (2) ENGINE STALL AND OVERTEMPERATURE. THE VARIATION OVER THE PAST 16 MONTHS IN THE SHUTDOWN RATE IS SHOWN. THE RATE PEAKED AT 6.7 SHUTDOWNS PER 1,000 FLIGHT HOURS EARLY IN JUNE. THEREAFTER THE RATE SHOWS A DECLINING TREND AND IS PRESENTLY AT 1.4 SHUTDOWNS PER 1,000 FLIGHT HOURS.

THERE HAVE BEEN 6 CASES OF MULTIPLE POWER LOSS IN FLIGHT, ONE OF WHICH RESULTED IN A 2 ENGINE-OUT LANDING. THIS OCCURRED ON 8/26/70 TO AIRPLANE TWA N93108. ENGINE NO. 2 STALLED AND WAS SHUT DOWN, FOLLOWED BY FAILURE OF A 5TH STAGE VARIABLE STATOR CONTROL LINKAGE BOLT ON NO. 4 ENGINE. IT TOO WAS SHUT DOWN. IN THE OTHER FOUR CASES OF MULTIPLE INFLIGHT SHUTDOWNS POWER WAS REGAINED ON ONE OR BOTH OF THE SHUT-DOWN ENGINES.

IN A RELATED EVENT, AIRPLANE N749PA TOOK OFF ON A THREE ENGINE FERRY FLIGHT ON 5/21/70 (NO. 3 ENGINE NOT OPERATING). DURING CLIMB THE NO. 4 ENGINE STALLED AND WAS SHUT DOWN. IT WAS RESTARTED FOR THE LANDING PHASE. NO CONTROL OR LANDING PROBLEMS WERE ENCOUNTERED.

7

POWER PLANT FIRES

- 25 IN FLIGHT POWER PLANT FIRES — JANUARY 1970 — APRIL 1971

- 7 POWER PLANT FIRES 1 MONTH PERIOD — MID MAY THRU MID JUNE 1970

- 1 POWER PLANT FIRE TO DATE 1971

- .36 FIRES/100,000 ENGINE HOURS, PERIOD 1/1/71 — 4/15/71, COMPARABLE TO OTHER ENGINES

- CONTINUING DOWN TREND WITH MODIFICATION INSTALLATIONS:

    IMPROVED SIDE COWL DRAINAGE

    IMPROVED ENGINE TO COWL SEALS

    REDUCTION OF IGNITION SOURCES

    REDUCTION IN LEAKS

8

A G E N D A

9:30	Introduction and Welcome
9:45	Boeing's Presentation - Operational Incidents
10:15	General Discussion of Operational Incidents
10:45	Pratt & Whitney Presentation of Major Engine Problems
11:15	General Discussion of Major Engine Problems
11:45	Boeing Presentation of Aircraft Problems
12:15	General Discussion of Aircraft Problems
12:30	Break for Lunch
2:00	Open Discussion of Additional Items
5:00	Close
5:30	Cocktails
6:00	Dinner

9

April 21, 1971

NOTE TO: D. E. Kinkel

SUBJECT: RESUME OF B747 INTRODUCTION PROBLEMS AND OPERATIONAL
SOLUTIONS

Per your request, the following is an outline of the significant problems encountere
in the first year of 747 operation. Also included are the operational adjustments
made to solve or alleviate these problems.

ENGINES
Problem: At random, engines would experience rapidly rising EGT with lagging
acceleration of N2. Some cases of engine overtemp before shutdown. This
problem continues today.

Action: Through a series of FIF's and AOM revisions, crews were educated on
the signs of incipient overtemp during start and given guidelines for determining
the necessity of early shutdown. As more was learned, start procedures were
changed to minimize the number of hot starts. When the -3A engine was intro-
duced, start procedures again had to be changed to account for the changed engine
characteristics.

Problem: When operating on the ground at idle thrust, engines would, on occasion,
go into a "silent stall" condition. EGT rises rapidly; N2 slows down; with no
external warning, crew would not be aware of this condition, possibly until the
engine had gone into overtemp condition.

Action: Crews were advised through FIF's and AOM procedures, of the necessity
for constant monitoring of EGT when operating on the ground. This was made
a specific duty of the FEO who was to pass this duty to the First Officer and
obtain acknowledgment if he had other essential duties to perform. This problem
was later alleviated by a switch which kept a 3.5 bleed open on the ground. The
crew monitoring is still important, since the switch has been known to fail, with
resulting engine overtemp if crew is inattentive. Crews have been instructed,
also, to maintain at least 62% N2 RPM during taxi.

Problem: High Altitude unrecoverable engine stalls, usually during deceleration.

Action: Installed throttle bars and pressure actuated warning light to assure place-
ment of bar above 29,000 feet. FIF's and AOM procedures specify use of bar
to prevent deceleration into stall range at altitude. Crews educated on causes
of stalls and instructed not to accelerate engine before they have stabilized
after thrust reduction. This prevents Bodie stall. Engines have been modified
to make this problem less severe. As a result we are changing the light to
actuate at 35,000 feet and adjusting procedures accordingly.

cont'd....

10

Page -2-   4/21/71

Problem: <u>Overtemps in reverse</u>. This usually occurs at high thrust due to ingestion, but can also occur (silent stall) when coming out of reverse.

Action: Several FIF's and AOM pages have been written to alleviate this problem. Procedures were tailored to keep reverse thrust below the surge line at some sacrifice in reverse effectiveness. Due to high incidence of overtemps, these procedures had to be re-emphasized and expanded at least twice. A reverser actuated bleed system (RABS) was installed on an expedite basis to increase surge margin and allow use of more thrust. Procedures were again changed to take advantage of this improvement. Reverse overtemps have remained high, however, due to RABS reliability problems and other stall conditions not cured by RABS. As a result we are babying the engines in reverse and are stuck with two procedures - one for RABS inoperative or on long, dry runways; one for poor stopping conditions with RABS operative.

Problem: <u>Engine vibration</u> occurs at random, usually during climb and is transmitted through the pylons into wing structure, and thence to the airframe. This is caused by fan tip stall when the fan case honeycomb is extensively smeared.

Action: Procedures were initiated instructing crews to reduce thrust until vibration disappears and maintain the thrust reduction until reaching cruise altitude and speed. Fan cases are changed when this occurs.

Problem: Engines exhibited excessive tendency to <u>lose oil in flight</u>, causing shutdowns and diversions.

Action: Data collection and analysis was initiated to determine if oil loss was real or indicated and to detect the cause. Special checking and reporting procedures were written for crews. Oil tank filling procedures were standardized and Maintenance procedures improved. New filler necks were added to tanks so more oil could be added.

Problem: Turbine <u>Blades were cracking</u> at a high rate.

Action: Crews were instructed to use takeoff thrust for no more than three minutes except in an emergency.

Problem: At least half of our engines operate at EGT levels in excessive of design at any given thrust level and ambient temperature. This has exacerbated the turbine blade cracking problem.

11

Page -3- 4/21/71

Action: Extraordinary efforts were expended to make demineralized water available at all 747 terminals. Instructions were issued that all 747 takeoffs at temperatures above 10°C were to be made using water injection unless physically impossible. JT9D-3A engines were de-rated to -3 thrust, wet or dry. Dry takeoffs were to be made using "packs on" performance with all packs actually off to reduce temperatures. Engines show no signs of running cooler this summer. We are, therefore, continuing and emphasizing these procedures. Climb thrust is also being reduced for the summer season.

Problem: Some engine fires were caused by ignition of residual flammable fluids in the nacelles.

Action: New baffles and drain holes were installed in nacelles to prevent fluid collection. Protective heat shields for temperature sensors were relocated to create usable nacelle temperature indications.

Problem: Failure of the condition actuator to operate the fuel control on engine shutdown caused at least one fire and several engine overtemps.

Action: Instructions issued to crews to monitor fuel flow on shutdown to verify actuator operation. FEO instructed to close fuel valve manually on any shutdown due to overtemp. Some aircraft have been modified so that the fuel valve is closed automatically at the same time the start lever is placed to cutoff. Due to evidences of failure of this automatic system crew procedures have been retained. Pan Am Operations has suggested changes to the automatic system which BACo will incorporate to increase reliability.

Problem: At random, a water injection valve will remain fully or partially open. When water pumps are turned on prior to takeoff this results in "drowning" of the engine and flameout at idle thrust.

WATER SURGING CREATES UNEQUAL THRUST

Action: Through FIF's and AOM material, crews were instructed on when to look for flooding, and what the indications would be. Procedures called for turning off water followed by a shutdown and relight if the condition did not recover.

LANDING GEAR

Problem: At random, brakes would release at low taxi speeds causing collision hazard. This was due to failures in the tilt switch input to the Anti Skid.

Action: FIF and AOM instructed crews to turn Anti Skid off whenever clear of the operating runway. This condition still exists.

12

Page -4-   4/21/71

Problem: Anti Skid braking system has long computation times on slippery runways. This results in time delay for application of optimum braking. Some pilots, thinking brakes had failed, switched to alternate brakes or turned off Anti Skid.

Action: FIF's and AOM instructions highlighted the situation and specified application of full and constant braking on a slippery surface. The dangers inherent in pumping the brakes causing recomputation were pointed up.

Problem: At start of takeoff, several pilots experienced severe directional excursions, causing aborted takeoffs. Conditions varied. It was found that there were several mechanical difficulties that could have caused these problems. It was also found that the 747 has more of a tendency to "weather cock" into the wind than previous aircraft. The airplane is also more sensitive, in the directional plane, to the application of asymmetric thrust. These factors could have caused some of the problems on slippery runways.

Action: Nose gear steering valves were modified. Cable rigging techniques were changed. Crews were alerted to the mechanical and aerodynamic problems by FIF's and AOM text.

Problem: There was concern about the possibility of body gear steering unlocking at high speed causing an undesired lateral translation.

Action: The condition of unlocked body gear was added to the takeoff warning horn. Later airplanes have a switch which centers and locks the body gear whenever rudder pedal is applied past 12°. This will be retrofitted.

Problem: If body gear strut extension is inadequate, the body gear can damage the load evener system in a turn. This will cause loss of hydraulic fluid, necessitating body gear removal for repair.

Action: By FIF and AOM text FEO's were instructed to check evener system servicing and strut extension on every preflight check.

FLIGHT CONTROLS
Problem: On at least two occasions segments of trailing edge flaps left the airplane in flight. Fatigue cracks later turned up in the flap track mechanisms on the fatigue test model at BACo.

Action: By FIF and AOM text crews were advised to use 25° flap for landing unless 30° was absolutely required. The use of 30° necessitated a lengthy inspection and subsequent delay potential. The restriction on use of 30° flap was later raised only to speeds above 140 kns. Aircraft are undergoing flap track modification which will soon allow unrestricted use of normal flaps.

13

Page -5-   4/21/71

Problem: It was found that the wing flap canoe fairings could disengage from their rollers on landing touchdown with flaps set at 25° or less. This resulted, on another carrier, in loss of a canoe in flight. This will not occur at 30° flap.

Action: By INTAM and FIF crews were instructed to use 30° flap where possible under existing restrictions. Flaps were to be left in the extended position and inspected if the landing had been made at 25°.

Problem: There were a number of cases of flickering of the Rudder Ratio warning light. This light warns of a disagreement between positions of the two rudder ratio actuators.

Action: Warning light tolerances were widened to prevent nuisance flickering. An airplane modification shut off power to the actuators when on ground power to prevent overheating.

Problem: If the Autoland system is engaged while maneuvering in the lateral plane the steady red Autopilot Warning Light will illuminate and the automatic pilot will disengage on final approach.

Action: By FIF and AOM text, crews were advised to engage the Autoland system in steady state condition. Trouble shooting procedures were recommended if light should illuminate.

FUEL SYSTEM
Problem: Undesired fuel transfer between tanks occurred at random, due to failure of fabric intertank dams.

Action: Metal dams are being installed as a permanent fix. An interim fuel usage procedure was established by FIF and AOM to control the problem.

Problem: Several instances occurred of partial thrust loss or unstable thrust after high altitude operation.

Action: Procedures were initiated for more frequent use of fuel heat than is called for by Boeing.

INSTRUMENTS
Problem: The indications on the HSI glide slope bar were unreliable with the landing gear up. This was due to antenna location. ILS

Action: Crews were advised by FIF of the problem and ILS approach procedures modified to extend landing gear early in the approach.

14

Page -6-   4/21/71

The markings on the ADI spheres were considered inadequate. Pitch
~e not bold enough, numbers were too small and roll bars were too
~ adequate attitude guidance.

he sphere was redesigned completely by Pan Am and put into producti

ANEOUS

A low frequency vibration in the number 2 pack ram air inlet system
jectionable rumble.

rocedures were initiated by FIF for manual control of inlet door to
the vibration in the effective range.

There were several instances of inadvertent deployment of the Main
r evacuation slides. This was usually done at the blocks by non-fligh
when the doors were left in Automatic.

rocedures were changed so that Flight Service personnel would place
in Auto after leaving the blocks, and back to manual before arriving at
. DOOR MANUAL/AOTC ACTUATING REDESIGNED-RETCG

There has occurred an inordinately high rate of generator bearing

n auxiliary bearing has been added to the generators, as well as a
ailure Detector Light. Procedures were initiated for operation on the
bearing.

Paul Roitsch

15

June 29, 1970

EXCESSIVE BOEING 747 COSTS

Introduction

The unusual problems encountered with the 747's
(including the JT9D engine) have resulted in heavy excess
costs, which are continuing. It is important that these
be identified, related to specific causes and measured,
in order to support claims for damage for breach of contract. This requires that relevant records be made and
maintained.

The purpose of this memo is to summarize,
primarily for the Operations Department, the major possible areas of claim, the types of cost involved, and the
records which might be required. This is a preliminary
listing, which will be reviewed and may be modified in
the light of analysis of the value and sufficiency of the
data, practical problems in its collection, and continuing
developments with the equipment.

We have made no attempt to deal with claims
which may arise under normal warranties, or any resulting
disputes, which we assume will be diligently pursued.
However, care should be taken in handling warranty claims

16

[PAN AM LETTERHEAD]

March   , 1972

Chairmen of the Board
The Boeing Company and
United Aircraft Corporation

Dear Sirs:

As I know you have been aware for some time,
Pan Am's experience with the 747 aircraft and the JT9D
engine has been quite disappointing in many respects.
You will recall that at the time of initial delivery of
the first aircraft in December 1969 it was recognized
that the aircraft failed to comply with certain of the
more important performance guarantees of the contract.
These problems were to have been resolved completely by
March of 1971; but they have not been, and it is perfectly clear that there is no prospect in the near future
that they will be.

The aircraft's engines, of course, have been a
source of extreme concern right from the beginning. Fore-
most among the problems has been the extraordinarily high
rate of fuel consumption, far beyond the specifications
which were a part of our original agreement. This of
course has required Pan Am to incur extraordinarily high

17

SCHEDULE OF DAMAGES
THRU MARCH 1972

I.   Cost of excess fuel consumed, as
     well as additional crew and mainten-
     ance costs, due to failure of air-
     craft and engines to comply with
     certain performance guarantees and
     fuel consumption specifications. $2,500,000

II. Costs incurred due to extraordinary
     and unanticipated rate of engine
     removals due to failure of aircraft
     and engines to comply with certain
     performance guarantees, and the
     effects of defective materials,
     workmanship and design. $12,575,000

III. Costs incurred due to delays, turn-
     backs, cancellations of flights,
     etc. due to failure of aircraft
     and engines to comply with certain
     performance guarantees and the
     effects of defective materials,
     workmanship and design. $3,100,000

IV. Costs incurred due to the effects
     of defective materials and workman-
     ship utilized in and defective de-
     sign of the Multiplex System. $3,000,000

V.   Damages incurred due to late delivery
     of the:

         A. Aircraft   210,000

         B. Spare Engines   240,000
                                                 $21,625,000

18

DATE: ___6/17/70___

LAST REPORT ___6/15/70___

JT90 STATISTICS

Total Engine Hours to Date	63,134
(Since Last Report)	1,686
Total Unscheduled Removals to Date	86
(Since Last Report)	1
Current Removal Rate per 1000 hours	1.31
(Last 3 months)	
Total Inflight Shutdowns	28
(Training not Included)	
Current Shutdown Rate	1.55%
Total Delays due Engines	51
Current Delay Rate	2.82%

Engines on Hand

	Installed*	Available Spares	Repair or Overhaul
-3	20**		
-3A	56	2	48
TOTAL	76	2	48

	Delivered to Date	Projected Total
Total Owned by PAA	114	143
Pool Engines on Loan	11	12
TOTAL	125	155

Number of engines exposed to sideplate rivet failure	101 (39 on A/C)
Accomplished	17 (15 on A/C)
Other HPT modules in process	30
Number of engines requiring N2 Tach Bearing	72
Accomplished NOTE: PAA Maintenance is not doing on campaign basis since new bearing has failed. Will incorporate new bearing on attrition basis.	
Engines requiring TSFC Improvements	125
Accomplished	0
Engines affected by ERP+ (-3 to -3A Conversion)	41
Completed	6
Balance Remaining	35 (16 @ P&W)

+ERP - Engine Recovery Program
**Including one BOAC loan engine.
NOTE: PAA has 2 engines of 39 requiring new HPT for wet operation.

PAN AMERICAN WORLD AIRWAYS

19

SUMMARY OF JT9D ER's FOR SUMMER '71

CAUSE OF REMOVAL	JUNE	JULY	AUGUST	TOTAL
I. FIRST STAGE TURBINE BLADES				
A. Cracked U-700 vented 1st turbine blade	9	13	17	39
B. Broken/failed PWA 1455 vented 1st turb blade		2	2	4
C. Broken/failed U-700 vented 1st turb blade	2		1	3
D. Cracked non-vented 1st turbine blade	1			1
E. Sub-total/removal rate/1000 hrs.				47/.42
II. HOT SECTION-GENERAL				
A. Cracked Borescope Boss		3	5	8
B. EGT limited	4	3	1	8
C. Burned 1st NGV	4	1	2	7
D. Suspect failed 2nd turbine blade			3	3
E. Combustor distress	1			1
F. LPT anti-rotation pin wear	1			1
G. Sub-total/removal rate/1000 hrs.				28/.25
III. TOTAL HOT SECTION REMOVALS/REM RATE/1000 HRS.				75/.67
IV. COMPRESSOR FAILURES				
A. Sixth stage blade	2	1	7	10
B. Cracked IGV	1	2		3
C. Second Blade	1		1	2
D. Suspect 15th stator vane			1	1
E. Sub-total/removal rate/1000 hrs.				16/.14
V. COMPRESSOR STALL				
A. Overtemp in reverse	1			1
B. Overtemp during taxi	1			1
C. Overtemp at ramp - PAA responsibility			1	1
D. Sub-total/removal rate/1000 hrs.				3/.027
VI. MISCELLANEOUS				
A. Oil leaks	1		2	4
B. N2 tach bearing failure		1	2	3
C. Plating on 2nd turb disc, precautionary removal due PWA recommendation		3		3
D. Condition motor - Boeing responsibility	1		1	2
E. High vibration		1		1
F. N2 limited (EVC trim)	1			1
G. FOD			1	1
H. Fan blade tab lock not properly installed allowing fan blade to fail-PAA responsible			1	1
I. Compressor failure due screwdriver left in engine at manufacture. PWA responsibility	1			1
J. Sub-total/removal rate/1000 hrs.				17/.15
VII. Total/Removal Rate/1000 Engine Hours	32/.92	31/.79	48/1.25	111/.99

20

51464362R00055

Made in the USA
Lexington, KY
24 April 2016